Bruno Mars

Author: Strand, Jennifer.

Lexile Value: 460L

Bruno Mars

Jennifer Strand

abdopublishing.com

Published by Abdo Zoom™, PO Box 398166, Minneapolis, Minnesota 55439. Copyright © 2017 by Abdo Consulting Group, Inc. International copyrights reserved in all countries. No part of this book may be reproduced in any form without written permission from the publisher. Abdo Zoom™ is a trademark and logo of Abdo Consulting Group, Inc.

Printed in the United States of America, North Mankato, Minnesota
092016
012017

THIS BOOK CONTAINS RECYCLED MATERIALS

Cover Photo: Dan Hallmann/AP Images
Interior Photos: Dan Hallmann/AP Images, 1; S. Bukley/Shutterstock Images, 4, 8; Joe Giddens/
PA Wire URN:20318544/Press Association/AP Images, 5; Zoia Kostina/Shutterstock Images, 6–7; Seth Poppel/
Yearbook Library, 7; Shutterstock Images, 9, 10; Bryan Bedder/Getty Images, 10–11; Helga Esteb/
Shutterstock Images, 12; A. G. Wilson/Shutterstock Images, 13; Kevin Terrell/AP Images, 14–15; Ben Liebenberg/
AP Images, 16; Matt Sayles/Invision/AP Images, 17; Alessandra Della Bella/Keystone/AP Images, 18; Frank Micelotta/
Invsion/AP Images, 19

Editor: Emily Temple
Series Designer: Madeline Berger
Art Direction: Dorothy Toth

Publisher's Cataloging-in-Publication Data
Names: Strand, Jennifer, author.
Title: Bruno Mars / by Jennifer Strand.
Description: Minneapolis, MN : Abdo Zoom, 2017. | Series: Stars of music |
    Includes bibliographical references and index.
Identifiers: LCCN 2016948677 | ISBN 9781680799187 (lib. bdg.) |
    ISBN 9781624025044 (ebook) | 9781624025600 (Read-to-me ebook)
Subjects: LCSH: Mars, Bruno, 1985- --Juvenile literature. | Musician--United
    States--Biography--Juvenile literature. | Singers--United States--Biography--
    Juvenile literature.
Classification: DDC 782.42164092 [B]--dc23
LC record available at http://lccn.loc.gov/2016948677

Table of Contents

Introduction

Bruno Mars is a singer and songwriter.

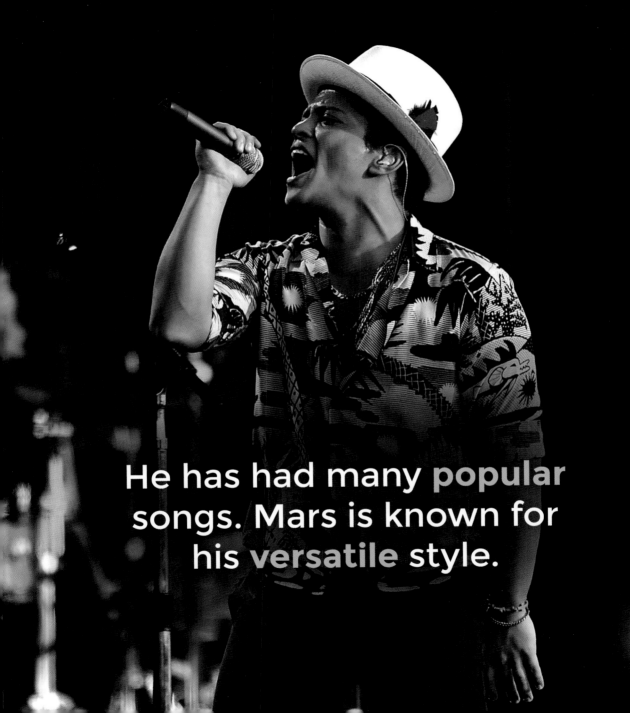

He has had many **popular** songs. Mars is known for his **versatile** style.

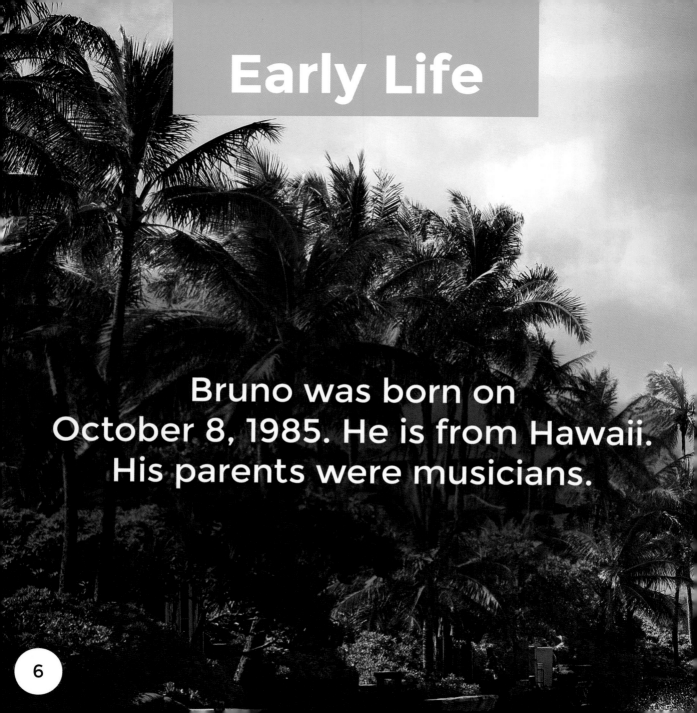

Early Life

Bruno was born on October 8, 1985. He is from Hawaii. His parents were musicians.

He started **performing** with them when he was four years old.

Rise to Fame

Mars wrote songs. He used many styles of music.

But no one would hire him to
make an **album**.

Instead Mars worked as a music **producer**. He helped other musicians make songs.

Sometimes he sang with them.
Many of the songs became hits.

In 2010 Mars
helped make a song.

Cee Lo Green
performed it.
It was a huge hit.

Then Mars
recorded his
first album. It had
many hit songs.
It sold more than
5 million copies.

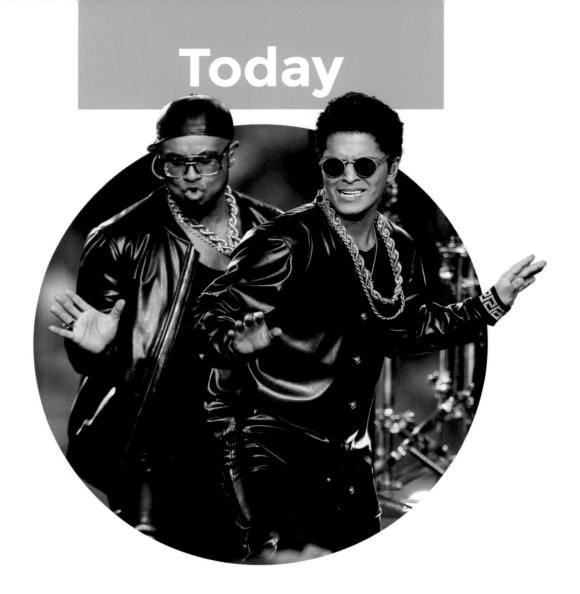

Mars is known for his dancing and sense of style.

People often compare him to pop stars from the past.

He **released** another album in 2012.
People liked his songs.

Mars continues to write music for himself and other musicians.

Bruno Mars

Born: October 8, 1985

Birthplace: Honolulu, Hawaii

Known For: Mars is a famous singer and songwriter.

Key Dates

1985: Peter Gene Hernandez Jr. is born on October 8. He is nicknamed Bruno. He later performs as Bruno Mars.

2005: Mars forms a songwriting and producing team.

2009: "Right Round" is released. It is Mars's first songwriting hit.

2011: Mars wins a Grammy Award.

2012: Mars releases his second solo album, *Unorthodox Jukebox*.

2015: Mars performs during halftime at the Super Bowl.

Glossary

album - a collection of music.

performing - doing something in front of an audience.

popular - liked by many people.

producer - someone who is in charge of making a music album.

released - made available to the public.

versatile - able to do many different things well.

Booklinks

For more information
on **Bruno Mars**, please visit
booklinks.abdopublishing.com

Z_Qm In on Biographies!

Learn even more with the Abdo Zoom
Biographies database. Check out
abdozoom.com for more information.

Index